Silent Voices

Poems

Rohit Shetty

First Step Publishing
Paving Ways For New Writers

Silent Voices

Poems

Rohit Shetty

Publishing
Paving Ways For New Writers

Second Edition by First Step Publishing 2019
303 Garnet Nirmal Lifestyles Ph 2
Behind Nirmal Lifestyles Mall
LBS Marg Mulund West
Mumbai 400080
E-Mail:- info@firststepcorp.com

Editorial / Sales / Marketing Office at
303 Garnet Nirmal Lifestyles Ph 2
Behind Nirmal Lifestyles Mall
LBS Marg Mulund West
Mumbai 400080

Paperback ISBN: - 978-93-83306-48-0
Book Editor: Rohit Shetty
Typeset in Book Antique.

Price: INR 150

Dedicated to my mother
Smt Jaswinder Shetty

About the Author

Born and brought up in Mumbai, Rohit Started writing at an early age of 11 years. Being an introvert person Rohit used to pen down his emotions in rhythmic form which turned to poetry. Being the youngest in the family Rohit was a pampered kid. After completing his studies Rohit joined his family business for while and post that ventured out to work in various companies. As far as writing is concerned Rohit loved writing and still writes as a hobby.

As far as his credentials is into writing, Rohit has bagged many awards. He has received 2 National awards and a couple of international awards in his kitty. Rohit has also been felicitated by Ex MLC Mr Charan Singh Sapra and MPCC president Mr Manikrao Thackrey in 2012 and 2013. Rohit has also received an appreciation letter by PM Narendra Modi in which he has congratulated Rohit for his work in literary domain by helping Indian writers to showcase their talent on international domain.
Rohit quotes his journey of writing as a method to study; remembering formulas and

events in a rhythmic way, to penning down unspoken emotions; from being publically ridiculed, to having published over 7 titles now available internationally.

Life is a journey,
With mountains and valleys.
Many forget the reality of life
These are the spots where tourist rally.

Rohit Shetty

You can get in touch with Rohit Shetty with your reviews at
Email: rohitnshetty@gmail.com
Twitter Handle: rohitnshetty
Facebook: www.facebook.com/rohitnshetty

Table of Contents

Today Is A New Day

The sun is shining, the sky is blue
There is a new dawn for me and you
With every dawning of the sun
New possibilities have just begun
With every day of morn
Fresh opportunities have been born
So what if the day was cloudy
Tomorrow will be fine
No one has ever failed kept
A happy state of mind
The longest journey taken
Starts from a single mile
And one day at a time will change
The worthless to worthwhile…

A Caged Spirit

A beautiful princess
Is trapped in a cage
So much in sorrow
So much in rage

She can't get out
Or so it seems
She needs to love
She needs to dream

But how to open
That sealed door
There must be a way
For hers to soar

A key somewhere
That she must find
But where to look
Or find a sign

She ponders this question
Day and night
But always the answer
Is out of sight

A knight rides by
And sees her there
She thinks he is another
That will not care

She turns away
And starts to cry
And shouts to the heaven
Why? Why? Why?

I've always been gentle
I've always been kind
Why do I suffer?
Why must I be blind?

The knight dismounts
And falls to his knees
In front of the cage
And says "Princess Please…"

"I'm the one
Who has sought you so long
Let us talk for a while
Let me sing you a song."

Through many long nights
They would walk and listen
Till the morning dew
Would start to glisten

They woke one morning
And knew it was true
That love was blossomed
And hope renewed

"I'll find a way"
He said to his bride
To open this door
And cast it aside

"And when I do so
You are free Never again
Will there be the need for the key."

"You'll always be cared
You'll always be loved
I swear on my soul
On all that's above."

He reached the door
And pulled on its latch
But the door would not give
For his strength was of no match

"We must wait for a while
Until the hour is right
Time must pass
Until we see light."

"I can wait no longer"
She spoke with a tear
"It has been too many hours
Too many years."

"My heart is weary
And longs to be free
My strength has left me
But I'll wait with thee."

"If you promise to love me
And stay by my side
One day I'll join you
And away we'll ride."

"I need you, my princess,
And with you I'll stay

For as long as it takes
For us to see that day."

"And when that day comes
And we are as one
Our joy will embrace us
Like the warmth from the sun."

"And never again
Your heart will be weary
Your eyes will be bright
Your smile will be cheery."

"I'll complete you
As you complete me
And our love will continue
Unbridled... And Free."

Or Is It Too Late?

So many times I thought of the day
When you held my hand
And I walked away

The pain in your eyes burned through me then
When I close my eyes I see it again

A love so young, so unbridled and raw
Being trapped and confused was all that I saw
How could I know how I feel today?
When I closed the door on your heart
And walked away?

Years went by and we both moved along
While part of my heart was still singing a song

Then I saw you again
And now I can see
The same eyes, the same heart
Looking right back at me

You hold me so close, I'm afraid to let go
To lose you again? How do I know?
But here you are now
You are with someone new

Does she hold you and kiss you
And feel like I do?
Faced with options
You know you must choose
Well it works with this time
Or will we lose?
Is it all about timing?
Or about fate?
Together again?
Or is it too late?

The Key To My Heart

I closed the door upon my heart & wouldn't let
anyone   in
I'd trust & loved only to be hurt that would
never be

I locked the doors & threw the keys as hard as I
could
Love would never enter again; my heart was
closed for good

Then you came into my life & made me change
my mind
Just when I thought that little key was
impossible to find

That's when you held out your hands &
proved I was wrong
In your hand was the key, the key to my heart
You had it all along

A Being With No Heart

You liked my poems
As they touched your...
Heart.
Which I am surprised now to know
As did you ever have a Heart?
Heart which feels
The pain
Breathes the air of love
As it lets thoughts inside
Since it was missing something
For it was alone
Being just one
Which all does make sense
If the heart is existent
Which I doubt is present in you
As you turned out to be a brick
Of stone
Which had decided to not let in
Any fresh air of love
For you had forgotten breathing
As the heart in you was stolen
Before I could reach it
And love you
Which is something I realize now
For only a stone cannot hear

The feelings
As it's hearing less
And blinded by the falsehood
Of what you define as truth
For it suits you
Which proved I was wrong
As I considered you
A human to be.

A Smiling Face

A smiling face always wins,
The frowns over to your side.
There's nothing like a toothy grin,
To make a scowl go hide.

A smiling face brightens up,
The darkest night around.
Dancing round with the kitchen mop,
Dispelling ugly frowns.

A smiling face chases winter,
From the human face,
Nevermore will you be bitter,
There's nothing it can't erase.

So wear a smiling face,
Everywhere you go,
It really is an acquired grace,
It's just as good as gold.
A GIRL THAT WEARS ON HER FACE.

For The Every First 'Hello' There's A Last 'Goodbye'

Promise me when our time has ended
The tears, broken heart & sorrows have
mended
When we say our last goodbye
And there's no more tears left to cry
Promise me that you'll keep our memories
alive
For someone new might soon arrive
For parting is the price we must pay
We loved each other and now go our separate
ways
I feel something is missing, when you walked
away alone
That night I sat waiting by the phone
But you won't be calling, there's no more you
What we had is gone, no longer shared by you
What we had is gone and no longer shared by
two
The spark is out, fire extinguished and gone
The love isn't personal; it's for whomsoever
comes along
But please promise me now while we are on
neutral grounds

That you'll dwell on our memories when the
mood comes along
For I'm tough, strong & promise not to cry
Because I know
For the every first "Hello" there's a last
"Goodbye"

Nothing But A Shadow...

Here we are walking
Yet not talking
Silence, silence

We've grown apart
Yet here we are
Walking, but not talking

We are together
Yet far apart
Silence, silence

I watch our shadows
With a sour look
Slipping farther apart

This cannot be
What happened to you and me
Silence, silence

What happened over the summer
You found a job
And we stopped seeing each other

I wish our shadows would be close again
Like when you and me were best friends
Silence, silence

Tear In My Eye

Walk out of that door behind me,
Don't ask me for my leave,
Though I may live in a hell of pains,
But thou shalt no more deceive.

'Coz if dreams must be shattered,
And my heart must be broken,
Then, 'tis all better be done,
'Ere the Morrow sees the Sun.

Go, your true love awaits you,
Go, he loves you more,
Go, for I shall survive again,
As I did, once before.

And if I may fail to live without you,
Then I'd be content to die,
With an image of your smiling face,
On the TEAR in my eye...

The Running Train

As the train moves and the sun rises…
I inch closer to the one I love…
The peal of time when the wind is in the air…
Is the same as it was in the month of
December…

The air that made me felt the warmth of her
hand
Despite nobody sat next to me in the moving
train…
The clouds that kissed the mountains…
And with sun all its radiance looked upon…

It made me miss the way we kissed…
And the way we feared as anybody moved
along…
As the engine neared the station…
My eyes began to glow like the old bulb on the
pole…

The place where I landed was never where she
was…
But it made me feel somewhere she was
around…

And with the hope she would come here for a day…
I see clouds in the skies even in the month of May…

Somewhere she lay dipped in pain…
And I far enough to hear her scream…
Holy shit! What happens to the weather whenever I am sad…
The winds baffle…The papers fly… and here comes the rain again!

A Beautiful Sight

Sitting in the valleys wild
I saw a joyful dream;
There was wonderful scenery
Full of trees and a stream.

In the form of a rivulet
Flown down to join the sea;
At the time to sunset
Humming were the bees.

It became night, wonderful was the sight
The moon rose bright and white;
I felt like that,
I have never seen such "a beautiful sight"

A Lesson Learned Too Late

I was once the little boy
Sitting in a classroom,
Staring at the clock
And wondering
When time would fly by.
Life, it seems,
Is not without irony.
For now I am the little man
Sitting in an empty home,
Wondering if had I listened
to that teacher in that classroom,
Would I know where
My time flew away?

A Life That I Took Away

Tears falling down my face As I look at her
Wisps of hair blowing on her face The etching
of worries clearly seen But a smile just for me
A recall of good times and bad Seeing what I
remembered
And now remembering what I see I see a
girl... I see a friend
I want to give her a beautiful life But she is
ready to go... I know
I hope it isn't too late to give her the life A life
that I took away

A Lonely Tear

A lonely tear falls down
A smile turns to a frown
Trickles down the cheek
Does not make you weak

A lonely tear escapes
A lifetime of mistakes
A sad and lonely heart
Others broke apart

A lonely tear is dried
So many nights it cried
A friend reached out his hand
And tried to understand

The lonely tear is gone
Life will carry on
With love from a friend
The lonely tears will end

A Person Like You

A person like you so sweet yet so fair
A person like you is very rare
A person like you is the angel to my eye
A person like you for whom I would die

A person like you makes all dreams come true
A person like you turns my grey skies blue
A person like you fills me with joy
A person like you makes me want to be your
boy

A person like you sets my heart free
A person like you spreads your wings and
saves me from a tree
A person like you makes me fall in love
A person like you flies higher than a dove

A Poem For You...

I write a poem for you today,
to get a place in your heart forever
A poem that could tell you my love for you
I write my poem with emotion and affection
for you to understand my deep thoughts for
you
A poem to love and a poem to understand its
soul
A poem to enjoy and a poem to understand its
happiness
A poem to think and a poem to understand its
way of life
A poem to learn and a poem to understand its
content
A poem to sing and a poem to understand its
melody
A poem to cry and a poem to understand its
sorrow
There are poems I have written but this is
especially for you
The poem could tell you how important you
are for me
The words come out freely from my mind to
write this poem
But there are no words to find my love for you

Those words cannot be missed as I miss your
love today
Let me have all those words put into my heart
and say I love to write a love poem for you

Addicted To Love

Listening to soft waves
I'm standing by the sea
Just dreaming about those moments
If you were here with me

Dreaming about you
I'm strolling by the bay
I just want to know how
To pass this lonely day

The sunset and the waves
These cold winds remind me of you
Don't know what's happening to me
Can anyone give me a clue?

I believed... I was in love
But I was never so sure
But I know something is happening to me
Something that has no cure

If this is love, what's happening to me?
And everyone around feeling the same
Then I should say I'm addicted to love
And it's just her to blame

All I Can't Say

There are so many words I cannot say,
When I look into your eyes.
I want to be able to tell you one day,
But I'm left speechless every time that I try.

You must have stumbled across the key,
And discovered so much more.
You found a hidden place in me,
You found my heart and opened the door.
And I cried in pain
of losing my dear friend.

Will it ever be the same again?
If it passes, will it be the end?
I realized it was worth so much,
As I lie in bed that night.
So I allowed my soul to be touched,
Without even putting up a fight.
Are my eyes deceiving me,
When I see you standing there?
Are you playing games,
Just to prove I care?

You speak my name in a prelude,
In a reference to love,
With such loving attitude,
as if it were a message from above.
With the palms of your hands
Pressed firmly against mine,
A white dove's lands,
And the sun begins to shine.

Someday I will see,
Though that day has not come yet.
You'll say you love me,

But will you ever forget?
If that happens and my spirit dies,
If my emotions drop,
Will you want to hold me when I cry?
Or will the love just suddenly stop?
We can't expect to fall in love and never cry.

You'll stay and play your part,
But after the beauty starts to die,
Will your footprints still be on my heart?
Though it would be hard to say goodbye,
Your friend I'll always be,
As long as we always try,
To keep the friendship between you and me.

The letter I will not send
Will casually inquire,
How could you have brought it to an end?
I was your one desire.
After this life is over,
You'll be one person I know I'll miss.

It'll be too late to start over, and so I leave you
with
This...
I'll hold you for a lifetime,
If you'll just hold my hand.
We could have a wonderful time,
In the days we have not yet planned.

All I See Is You

I remember us,
The way we used to be,
I'd hold you in my arms,
Your smile so sweet to me,

But now when I see you,
You look right through me,
I feel so alone now,
But when I close my eyes...

...All I see is you.

The love we used to share,
Gone up in whirl winds,
Will I ever love,
or ever live again?

I am tired of crying,
And I am done trying,
To remember all about you,
But when I close my eyes...

...All I see is you.

All the love I am sending,
The memories I won't sell,
I know there must be an ending,
To the story I will tell,

I dream only of your love,
And happiness in life,
I try not to think of you,
But when I close my eyes...

..All I see is you.

At First Sight

I remember the day when I first met you.
It seemed like yesterday when my heart was
blue.
The hard troublesome soul I hide away.
All the tears I once had are up in my mind.
The first time when my eyes first laid upon
you,
Through my heart, all I could feel was your
soul.
As the smile I see you opposing every day,
I would freeze up and have nothing to say.
Upon the stars that shine brightly at night,
The day when my heart went up was at first
sight.

Beyond Close Words

If you could number the pinholes
Punched in the darkness of the sky.
By the stars that float
Just behind its penetrated curtain.
Knowing that you are seeing
Only the closest and the bright.
While understanding the infinite numbers
of lights not yet seen.
Then you might begin to comprehend
all the words I have yet to speak to you.
Or why I look beyond the closest words
which you speak to me.
For beyond the veiled sounds of your voice.
There floats unspoken words of love.
Like Christmas lights scattered across a
seasoned night.
Punching holes in my darkness.
Is it any wonder?
That my gaze is upon you!

Bliss

My instincts blur,
As a void begins to fill.
One, that I try to conquer,
In my quest to hold still.

I don't feel pain.
But I want to heal.
There isn't anything to gain.
But I want to feel.

Escaping my misery,
With each passing thought.
I try and break free.
But my mind has me caught.

The light flickers,
As I begin to fade away,
Into the darkness that lingers.
Silently hoping, time will stay.

Enigma

An enigma you are, un-understood, unsolved
Crawling silently, a visitor uncalled
You come in and settle without a knock
And speak no words, there's nothing to talk

Face, body, colour, taste and smell you lack
Your presence is pregnant silence black
You look and find your image in my eyes
Slowly replaced by the vast skies

Wind of sorrow turbulent grips the sky tight
Poor sky is no match to the delirious might
It screams thunder and cries out rain
Then no wind or sky, only my trickling tears of
pain

I need a shoulder to lean and cry
And a hand to soothe my sigh
You've caused my heart's turmoil and
emptiness
I ask your identity, you say, "My name is
Loneliness".

Expression of drops...

Sometimes it rains from cloud,
Sometimes from eyes it comes out.
Few drops of water,
Have many ways to flow out.
Takes no reason,
Just falls down.
The all-time source,
Which is alive in the soul;
Somewhere eyes can't reach,
But there eyes can meet;
Just the pair of eyes,
Flows when misses somebody,
Or even get anybody.
By a love met, a mother, a father,
A son or a daughter;
As all alive has tears,
In their unique creature.
The love is expressed by tears.
Just like our Mom-The Earth,
Expresses feelings as rains... tears,
In joy sorrow or cheers...!

Fallen Leaves

I walk in a forest,
A forest that I have not seen before,
A forest that had utter darkness.
I began to walk into the deep shadows.
As the whispers of the death haunt my ears
By the time I saw the last leaves fall beside me,
I knew this is the end of my road.
Or is it?
Could it be a sign?
Of what the world might turn into or be?
I feel an emptiness of my heart,
That broke into tears.
Fallen Leaves...

For My Someone Very Special

For my someone very special
The one who warms my heart
The woman who takes all my little fears
And tears them apart
I just wanted to say, "I love you"
And thank you for being you
And after all that we have been through
I'm glad you still love me too
Because without you here
And I just couldn't live that way
I'll never forget the time we met
Uncertain of what lay ahead
But look at us now, we're going strong
Not forgetting all that we have said
We were meant to be, this isn't a dream
And in each other's arms we will stay
I know this is true because within myself
I love you more and more each day

Happiness Costs A Lot These Days!

Happiness costs a lot these days,
Nature can take it from us in many ways.
They'll be a lot of people to mock and sneer,
Sometimes they are your enemies
And sometimes your dears.
We have to keep going on this open road,
'cause we don't know when we might abode.
We have to climb every mountain and fall into
every
Stream
or we'll never get the chance to chase our very
own
Dream.
We have to follow every rainbow on our way,
And we'll find our happiness later one day.
So my friends find the smallest reason to smile
At the baby's yawn or their glowing eyes.
You can do it in many other ways,
And remember happiness costs a lot these days

Her Smile

One of those endless days began...
Meant exclusively to tire man.
I woke up to face this day;
Nothing new, just a rerun of yesterday.
Attending my lectures, meeting my friends;
Old books and faces, no new turns or bends.
I then walk my same old way;
Back home, another night to stay.
A car stops in front of me;
I look up, not expectantly.
A simple sight greeted my eye;
Beautiful enough to make me stop and sigh.
One little child looked out the window;
Smiling at everyone, be it a friend or a foe.
A smile full of enthusiasm and happiness,
Filling my heart, taking away my emptiness.
I didn't know her, probably never will...
but her smile is with me still.
I won't ever know why the smile showed;
For it to be shared was all that on that road
Or maybe a new toy brought about that smile...
Which makes me write this poem after all this
while.
Her unquestioning and innocent love for all
showed on

Her face;
Her cheerful face meeting my gaze.
O little child, you will never know;
That your face still doesn't let me be low

I'd Have To Be A Thief

Your lips, your eyes, your soul
Are like a work of art,
The most creative thing of all
Is your beautiful heart.

If you were a painting,
No colours could express
The beauty deep inside you,
A rainbow, nothing less.

If you were a sculpture
The clay could hardly make
Your figure of an angel
Without one mistake.

If you were euphony
No choir could really sing
All the beautiful music
Your eyes could possibly bring.

So here I am, an artist,
With inspiration beyond belief
But to capture such rare beauty,
I'd have to be a thief.

If Dreams come True...

If dreams come true,
The sky won't remain blue;
The sun won't remain hot,
And things wouldn't be bought.

If dreams come true,
Life would be fun;
The work left to do,
Would already be done.

If dreams come true,
There'd be miracles everyday;
Mysteries without a clue,
Perils holding sway.

If dreams come true,
Who knows what'll happen;
Man may have to rue,
The very existence of men.

So let the realm of fancy
Be open till we're asleep;
Let life not be chancy,
As we sow, let us reap.

If I

If I hugged you,
would you never let go?
If I kissed you,
would you cherish that moment?
If I reached for your hand,
would you take mine gently?
If I needed a shoulder,
would you let me cry on yours?
If I needed to talk,
would you really listen?
If I needed to scream,
would you do it with me?
If I needed to go,
would you come with me?
If I fell for you,
would you catch me?

If I Were A Poet

Like the chime when you hear
You see the wind
It's the smell in the breeze which tells me
When she is near
If I were a poet I would have compared
To a rose or an art her beauty unmatched
If I were a poet I would have said
Soul meets body with the touch of her hand
If I were a poet I would have known
When the winds were still she had gone. Alas!
As time flies
And her memories blur
The sound of her laughter
Drowns in the well of my tears
Her memories tingle
bells of my heart
Her kiss I remember
Still makes my heart flutter

In The Pages Of Time

In the pages of time
You can see your next coming morning.
Full of sunshine madness.

That will give you a smell of green grass,
The sunshine, it's like a promise,
Like a respond, like a wild forest
With deep bright dreams.

The sunshine that gives you a
Natural existence of appearance and hope

The invisible wind is touching the
Mind and your thought
Where lies the deepest melancholy
Served of music

With full of possibilities
Destined your way
Will probably come very soon
With miracles in pages of time

Journey Of Love

Two destined lovers met one day
Their love was fairy tale,
As she would often say:
"He's my loving Saviour
He's my strong white knight,
I'll love him until I die,
The love we share's so right."

Their love grew stronger
Their hearts became whole.
To others they were in-separable.
Their love came from their soul.

From day to day,
Their love stayed warm
Even through thick and thin,
Their love would not be torn.

He called her his princess,
His baby and his heart.
They pledged their love together,
And promised they'd never part.

Together they planned their future.
Together they planned their life.

They planned that they would marry
And she would be his loving wife.

Who would have thought?
Their clear blue sky,
Would turn black and grey?
Who would ever imagine?
Their love would drift away

Their love which came from heaven.
Had slipped before their eyes
Their love which once was warm.
Now slowly dies.

Their hearts were torn apart,
By life's everyday sins.
Now they are not together,
Their feared fate sadly wins.

But their love is still alive
The love within their heart.
Though they cannot rebuild
The love they felt at the start.

So now there is no end,
No key to set them free.
Living this life in misery
As their once true love
Is history.

Love At First Sight

Just strolling in the park
Something just made me smile
It wasn't someone's presence there
But just your face in my mind

It all happened when I first saw you
You looked so sweet and bright
I kept looking stunned at you
May be it was love at first sight

But then I thought it wasn't love
Just a feeling for a day or two
But days passed by... and you were still in
mind

I just dreamt about you... all day long
That smiling face of yours
And when you actually stood before me
I stood with a pause

I couldn't speak a single word
Just a few words... Hi There
And when you actually step back and go away
I feel next time I'll dare

Though that next day never came in life
Just nothing I could say
But yes… I should confess one thing
I dreamt about her all day.

Made For Each Other

If I feel that I like her
In case it seems that I love her
It is not because of her beautiful eyes
Or the pretty way in which smiles
It is not because of the way she walks
Nor it is the way that she talks

Or the way she dresses
And absolutely not because
Of her tricky glance
Well it is not because of her beautiful voice
Or her sweet singing
And of course not because of her crazy looks

That tears my heart apart
It is not her wit on the grin
That actually moves
Mountains and oceans apart

But if you ask me
That what's it then that
Makes it seem
That I like her, I love her
It is just because
She is made for me and I'm made for her.

More Than Words Can...

More than words can express,
Feelings can;
Love, though apart the affectionate
And tenderness of your love
Could be felt in the air.

Though not close to you,
I can still feel your touch
In the air,
As breeze goes by;

Though heartily apart,
I COULD FEEL
YOU CLOSE BESIDE ME.

That's why my love;
You're so precious
to me.

Never I Have Fallen

Your lips speaks off the sweetness
Your touch a cool caress
I'm lost in your magic
My heart beats within your chest
I think of you each morning
And dream of you each night
I think of your arms being around me
And cannot express my delight
Never have I fallen
But I'm quickly on my way
You hold my heart in your hand
That's never before given away
I wrote your name on the sand
But the waves washed it away
Then I wrote it in the sky
But the winds blew it away
So I wrote it in my heart
And that's where it will stay
I thought love was just a mirage of the mind
It's an illusion, its fake, impossible to find
But the day I met you I began to see
That love is real and exists in me

Nobody Sees A Broken Heart

That smiling face
Everlasting grace
Watching me play
And never grey
Sitting pretty all the time
Singing that tinkling rhyme
As If a sweet child
Going crazy and wild
Everyone cared
But no one dared
To ask me why
Is that I cry
Coz they have their own
Troubles to bemoan
So I smile a big smile
Taking off the pile
So they don't see my sorrow
Just the smile they will follow
Of life this is a part
Nobody sees a broken heart

Only Strangers Are Beautiful

Desires are immortal, Patience lasts forever
Desire shall make Love to Patience, Beauty
Will be born.
Beauty never dies, Beauty never grows.
Beauty never lies, Beauty never shows.
Rhythm of the Trees, Vision of the Bees.
Beauty is what the Beholder sees.
Happiness to a man, Tears of wisdom and pain
of a lady.
Uncertainty of a teenager.
Cheers of cheekiness and anger of a young
slim lady.
The Wink of a Lusty Eye, Breath of a Virgin's
Cry.
A semi-nude woman wet, confused or shy.
Honey on soft skin, sweetness of a woman's
kiss.
Beauty around us everywhere, Beauty we
succeed to miss.
God Created Man, God Created Beauty.
Man Mistook God, Man Mistook Beauty.
Beauty to me, is Poetry, so new, so true.
Only Strangers are Beautiful. Do I see a
stranger in
you?

Secret Admiration

All the days in my week,
I write the name I dare not speak.
My love, with charcoal hair,
My beloved, my despair.
All I, on earth, want is a chance,
To burn my urge by your mere glance.
Will you ever punish me, with the little ever
blink of your eyes,
A glimpse of which leaves me a frozen block of
ice.
By your glimpse for the shortest ever while,
Stretches on my face the biggest ever smile.
Thy thought, a softened touch, filled with love,
leaves me crushed each day,
With a withered tongue, a swallowed mind
and nothing ever to say.
Thee, nay thine eyes, broke each of my vein,
Which left me by your little arrows, right
through slain.
Why am I ever a slave to your spell?
Why must I ever worship you? I never tell…

Shatters Beneath The Splashes

I watch that single drop of rain trickle down
the broken glass

In which the image is sustained from being
shattered.

Slowly from which it started merges with
another and the rain does not stop.

Now not one but two drops conjoin as that
sharp edge cuts inward.

Soon to be set apart as room runs out I stretch
forth my hand waiting for a miracle

only to be succeeded with it slipping between
my fingers.

The glass falls, the rain drops and it shatters
beneath the splashes

Silence Echoes

Silence
Makes my heart break Silence
Love, does not make

Silence
Was it all just a terrible mistake?
Silence
Was love just a game, just fake?

Silence
Leaves me heartbroken Silence
Kills the feeling behind words unspoken

Silence
Has is a shield you hide behind Silence
Guards what's on your mind

Silence
Chills your heart's sound Silence
Love cannot silently be found

Silence
Has turned your dreams blind Silence
Is darkness in which you cannot find

Silence
Crushes the hopeful feelings that were kind
Silence
Of emptiness it did remind

Silence
Silence took all I sought to find Silence
Silence was hurtful and unkind

Silence
Will kill love before it ripens on the vine Love
will go silently
But it's lonely hurt will echo for all time

Smouldering Tears

Along that bay of eyes
Showering its dew over the cheeks
Believe me that will rise
Through the nights of several weeks

As when the smouldering turn
Into the wet shores, its memory flow
That makes a backwater to earn
A moment of life by which the heart grow

And tides of many beautiful times
Make a picture in the mind's television
All that rhythm and rhymes
Of melody of love has its wonderful season

That can provoke never-surfeited
Dreams and hopes to be still alive
And a solace that's not defeated
By the destinies blow but strive

On and on as long as the destination
Will not be reached, these are
The conditions that define a smallest tear
That come over eyes and leave a scar

Of the heart's wound, but the pain
The loneliness, feelings have no sound
If it has a voice in vain
Then not a single sorrow will surround.

The Moonlit Princess

Enticing an open eye,
Like the moves of an angelic dance,
As though painting someone's imagination,
Through open desires.

Helping a broken heart to strengthen,
As if time had begun from this moment,
And walking through every dreamlike ,
A stranger in paradise.

As though blooming from petals,
Crushing every dry autumn leaf,
With her pure feet,
In a saga of beauty.

As dainty as a deer,
As distracting as the new breeze,
As beautiful as every thought,
Is she.

In a peculiar heart,
Lives this princess ,
In every moment identified as the
The Moonlit Princess.

The Smile

A sarcastic irony.
Of depth it is of loss
While such does none,
of hollow it does burn.
Emotions concealed
Thus, a life of deceived reality.
It moves of no impetuous flow
shows a fraction of truth behold.
Should one see,
a facade burns to life
of slow track, one could wonder
reality...behind the smile.

Thinking About You

As usual alone one day I sat
Doing nothing in my flat
Gently from outside the air blew
And I just started thinking about you.

Came to my mind, you, the first day I saw
I was in a state that left a feel of awe
Moments had passed which were so few
That I had started thinking about you.

Many a time, we used to make time and talk
As well as hand in hand, catch up and walk.
It looked for a long time, each other we knew
Which at night, used to make me think about
you.

Life started to look so joyful and bright
especially when I had you by my sight.
Everyday looked, to offer, something new
All this was because I started thinking about
you.

Alas, unfortunately had to come a day
When you decided that you go your way.
What went wrong, I don't have a clue
Though always I was thinking about you.

Alone I walk and sit in the canteen
Where we used to meet and have fun umpteen.
Food as I try hard to eat and chew
Makes my mind start thinking about you.

Life now has become very bleak
As it's you whom I still seek.
Though in the bond has dried away the glue
it hasn't stopped my mind to think about you.

As I wander like a corpse
eyes gets moist and lets out sobs.
Anybody else I can't accept in lieu
as my mind will always think about you.

Acknowledgments

Being an introvert person, I found it very difficult to convey my messages or emotions to others. Most of the times in my childhood I used to be alone having very few friends; only the few of my age group then used to play cricket. I was not allowed by my parents to play football in the rain or in the mud as others used to play as I often fell sick due to the climate change. There were loads of things which I wanted to say but I couldn't say because of my nature. I began to become quieter. My parents got me a cycle at that time and I used to ride most of the time, neglecting my friends as well with whom I used to play cricket. It happened so that eventually everyone had a bicycle; we all used to ride our bicycles very fast in the complex where we stayed many of whom I'm in touch with even today.

When in the fifth standard I was losing on grades, one friend in particular helped me out by helping me remember things. He asked me to write and practice and try to write in short ways and in rhythmic ways so that it is easy to remember. While doing this once for a chapter in geography, it turned out to be a poem. And it started from there. I began to think if studies can be made in a rhythmic way, why not emotions, so I began to write whatever came in my mind, the messages or emotions that I couldn't convey were scribbled down. This continued till I reached the ninth standard.

It's during the vacation of the ninth standard that studies for the tenth standard begin. To improve my English and to clear doubts, rather loads of doubts, I used to go to an English Teacher who stayed in the same complex and was also our family friend. It was once while talking to her it came out of me that I used to write which was a well-kept secret till that time. She asked me to show some of my writing if not all. I selected five poems and took it along with me to her place and she started reading; she was one of the first to encourage me to start writing. Just once while surfing on the net in the year 2001 I stumbled across a website for a poetry contest. I entered it. Out of 3.1 million entries, my poem was qualified and was published in the International Book of Poetry, Maryland, USA, subsequently in the year 2004 three of my poems were published in the local edition of The Times of India. I was happy with my name being published in the press.

I would also like to thank my friends at one point of time who thought I cannot write and made fun of me, mocked me, and even laughed at me publically. I seriously thank them from the bottom of my heart; if it hadn't been for you guys I wouldn't have come so far. I would also like to thank my colleagues who persuaded me to write despite having quit writing at one time. They also gave me ideas about what to write over the phone and over the internet.

Last but not the least I would like to thank my parents for being there with me all the time through the thick and thin of my life.

This book is a very small part of the journey I have been through time.
Hope you like it.

www.ingramcontent.com/pod-product-compliance
Lightning Source LLC
Chambersburg PA
CBHW020516030426
42337CB00011B/414